Freedom
Through
Forgiveness

By
Nathan Daniel

Freedom Through Forgiveness

Copyright © 2007 by Nathan Daniel

Vision Publishing Services

ISBN # 1-931178-18-6

All Scripture quotations from the Bible
unless otherwise noted are from the New
American Standard Bible-Updated version.

Published by:

Vision Publishing
1115 D Street
Ramona, CA 92065
www.visionpublishingservices.com
1-800-9-VISION

Book Cover Art by
Benjamin Monson

Printed in Hong Kong

Table of Content

Nathan Daniel

Dedication Page

I dedicate this book to the three most important women in my life. First is my mother Clara who taught me to trust. I always knew she would at least listen and try to understand me when life seemed unfair and I was hurting. She was always tender, caring and gentle. Yes, she corrected me, but even then I felt understood and loved. I remember how she took the time to help me prepare for a school test that I just knew I was destined to fail but that with her help I actually aced. She also talked to me about the facts of life and how I must be the protector not only of my own virginity but also of the girl's. I later learned that her instruction in this regard was the true definition and purpose of godly masculinity and strength. She taught me the power of gentleness. I am so thankful that she opened her heart to me and taught me not to be afraid of being openhearted with God or my wife. Having known the heart of my mother makes me willing to fight every day to keep heart to heart with my wonderful wife. At times in my young life, when others misunderstood me and accused me of wrong doing, she listened and stood by my side and helped me appeal my case and win, and therefore helped me learn what King David meant when he wrote that God is the "lifter of my head."

The second woman in my life is my wonderful wife of thirty-four years, Wanda. As surely as Jesus has been my surgeon, she has been his faithful nurse, always by my side no matter what life dealt us. So many times I would have given up the fight had she not stood by faithfully, even though neither of us understood why the battle raged so long and so hard. She has truly been my helpmate. Without her support, I could not have come to the place of writing this book or staying with this kind of healing ministry. She has provided an oasis of love and laughter to which I could retreat from the battle, reminding me again and again that since He who sits in the heavens laughs, so should we too!

The third woman in my life is my precious daughter Charity, whom I am also getting to know as a co-laborer in the vineyards of the Lord. I have to thank Charity for two things. First, she was one of the Father's first messengers to innocently point out while walking beside me in freedom that I was living in a dark prison. Second, when she heard my message on forgiveness, she was willing to forgive me, her earthly father, for those failures of mine that had wounded her child heart.

It is my hope that each of you will be able to walk out of any darkness you might be in as I share with you the result of the lessons Father has taught me through my own struggles and those of others.

Recommendations

What a privilege it is for me to have this opportunity to recommend Nathan Daniel's book Freedom Through Forgiveness.

When I first read a rough draft of the manuscript, I could not put it down. I was personally impacted on many different levels. I so appreciated the straightforward way Nathan presented the keys to healing and freedom that he has discovered during his thirty-five years in ministry. He is wonderfully transparent as he shares his journey of being hurt then harboring unforgiveness towards the offending person. He is brutally and wonderfully honest because he loves people. Anyone who knows Nathan understands that the man has a passion to see the body of Christ healed, free and victorious. He longs for the church to walk in the fullness of all that God has for them.

In this book, you will learn effective, proven principals from the word of God, which can open even those prison doors that have long since rusted close. You will read testimony after testimony that bear witness to the powerful transformation that occurs in the human heart when these principals are applied. You will find hope, truth, life and the love of the Father.

Freedom Through Forgiveness is most excellent and I highly recommend it!

Rhonda Calhoun, author of *The Bride*

****

This book will prove to be a blessing for a lot of reasons. Let me list three.

It is written from a strong biblical perspective. The whole concept of being set free from brokenness or any sort of bondage is at the core of Gods word. Nathan Daniel is able to take this scriptural truth and make it extremely practical and applicable.

Secondly, this material comes from the heart of a true pastor. Nathan cares about people. He has spent his whole adult life ministering to people's needs. This material reflects a deep understanding of God's power to deliver all who are in need.

Thirdly, the whole book is filled with real life situations. Nathan shares a wealth of illustrative material which helps to authenticate both the need and the solution.

The book will encourage, inform and empower God's servants in ministry to help people get free from life's bondages. Forgiveness is from the heart of God.

C. Douglas White,
Founding Pastor of Restoration Church, Euless TX

****

Nathan Daniel's Freedom Through Forgiveness not only exposes the severity of unforgiveness, but also reveals the power of God to truly set the captive free. What Pastor Daniel shares is not just theory, but reality of what has been worked out in the trenches of pastoral ministry over thirty-three-plus years. I highly recommend this book for every believer.

Dick Dungan,
Founder of Rejoice Ministries

****

I have known Nathan Daniel for over twenty years. I have watched him grow in his calling and gift to the body of Christ. Nathan has a wonderful understanding of godly principles, especially as it relates to forgiveness. He has not only helped many at the church he pastors, but he has been used of the Lord in the body of Christ, both in the U.S. as well as overseas. Nathan, in his own personal life and experience, has walked through the principles he shares. Freedom Through Forgiveness is a must read for every serious disciple of Christ.

George Runyan
Director
City Church Ministries

****

The ministry of healing, especially the healing of damaged emotions has often been misunderstood and sadly misapplied. In light of present reality, that most new believers today come to the church with significant wounds from the past, healing and often deliverance is vitally needed. What is also needed is wise ministry, judiciously and effectively given to ensure proper care and healing of these precious wounded souls.

In Pastor Nathan Daniel's very practical book Freedom Through Forgiveness, the knowledge of the process of healing the soul provides the understanding necessary for effective healing ministry, leading to wisdom, or the ability for God's people to live out the principles of God's word effectively with joy. More than a good read, this is a most timely and helpful work for the body of Christ.

Stan E. DeKoven, Ph.D.
President
Vision International University--Education Network

****

Nathan Daniel

INTRODUCTION

The concepts in this book are practical and applicable. Though the process is never easy, God's healing power is available when we present to Him a willing heart. All the stories are about real people; however, their names, identities and circumstances have been changed to allow the focus to be on the point of application.

Learning Through My Own Heart

Many years ago, the Lord allowed me to be hurt in a church relationship. I was a pastor and loved my church, as pastors do. During that time, I was deeply hurt by the words and actions of one of the church's leaders. I did not realize how much I had been hurt, but the pain went very deep. Months later, I developed chronic back pain. Unaware of the relationship between my emotions and my bodily health, I began going to doctors to find medical answers to my back pain. The doctors took x-rays and ran tests but could not find anything physically wrong. I was unable to recall any incident of falling or lifting that might have caused the pain. One doctor finally prescribed pain medication, but even that did not provide much relief. As the months dragged on and the pain worsened, I eventually was unable to sleep on my back at night.

Gradually, other symptoms emerged. I would be overcome with waves of depression that caused me to withdraw from people. I wanted to spend most of my time alone because I felt safer. It seemed like I would be having a good day, and then an event or thought would trigger the depression. It was almost like something would cloak me, like the cloud over the head of the little cartoon character. I even withdrew from my young children who needed their daddy to love them and play with them. There were financial pressures because of the problems in the church. I felt like I was in a prison without bars, but a prison nonetheless.

This went on for two long years. I did not have anyone to talk to. I was a pastor. I was supposed to have the answers, but I did not. Nor did I know anyone who had been through something like this and was walking in freedom.

One day while I was alone with God, praying and studying the Word, I told Him that I realized I was in a spiritual prison and would do *anything* to get out. He showed me that there was anger and hatred in my heart. He also showed me that, if I would go to the church leader who had hurt me and ask him to forgive me for hating him, I would be set free. The idea of humbling myself before such a person was unappealing to me, but I did it because I so desperately wanted out of my prison.

I made the appointment and went to meet with the man. He had been my associate but was now the pastor of the church I had left. I asked him to forgive me for hating him. He said he forgave me then added that I did not know how to pastor a church. I wanted to smack him, but instead just got up and walked out. The depression lifted immediately, and within two days my back pain was also gone. I felt like a hundred pounds had been lifted off my shoulders. I could feel the blessed presence and freedom of the Lord again. The Holy Spirit, who is able to "pierce as far as the division of soul and spirit, of both joints and marrow, and able to judge the thoughts and intentions of the heart" (Hebrews 4:12), had cut into my heart and taken out the splinter. I only wished I had known to go to the Surgeon two years earlier.

Welcoming *THE* Counselor

Throughout this book, I hope to introduce you to the Holy Spirit as your Comforter, Counselor, Guide, Teacher and Helper. The night before He died, Jesus revealed the ministry of the Holy Spirit to His disciples, as seen in the following scriptures:

> *I will ask the Father, and He will give you another* **Helper,** *that He may be with you forever; that is the Spirit of truth, whom the world cannot receive, because it does not see Him or know Him, but you know Him because He abides with you and will be in you.* (John 14:16-17)

> *But the* **Counselor,** *the Holy Spirit, whom the Father will send in My name, He will teach you all things....* (John 14:26 NIV)

> *When the* **Helper** *comes, whom I will send to you from the Father, that is the Spirit of truth who proceeds from the Father, He will testify about Me....* (John 15:26)

> *But when He, the Spirit of truth, comes, He will* **guide** *you into all the truth; for He will not speak on His own initiative, but whatever He hears, He will speak; and He will disclose to you what is to come.* (John 16:13-15)

> *But the **Comforter**, which is the Holy Ghost, whom the Father will send in my name, he shall teach you all things, and bring all things to your remembrance, whatsoever I have said unto you.*
>
> (John 14:26 KJV)

Jesus described the ministry and person of the Holy Spirit in specific ways. He said that when He went to heaven to be with the Father, He would send the Holy Spirit to be "in them," not just with them, as was the case when Jesus was living among them. Jesus called the Holy Spirit *the* Counselor, not *a* counselor. When we ask Jesus to come into our hearts, forgive our sin and declare Him the Lord of our life, we receive the Holy Spirit *in* us. Therefore, we have access to everything that He does from within us. We indeed have the best Counselor in the whole world— the One who made us and knows us better than we know ourselves. Jesus also said that the Holy Spirit would be a guide to lead us into all truth, and that He would never lie to us. Jeremiah 17:9-10 is important because the Word tells us that "The heart is more deceitful than all else and is desperately sick; who can understand it? I, the LORD, search the heart, I test the mind, even to give to each man according to his ways, according to the results of his deeds" (NAS).

Much of the work of healing wounded hearts is inviting the Holy Spirit to bring His truth to places where we have believed or practiced a lie. The King James Version refers to the Holy Spirit as the Comforter. Jesus also said that the Holy Spirit is our Helper. The Holy Spirit is gentle and able to speak difficult things to us in a soft, loving way with the purpose of convicting us of sin and causing us to want to turn from it.

Psychology is often helpful in the realm of helping people find out what is broken inside them. However, in the ministry of healing wounded hearts, we do not rely only upon our mental capabilities. Instead, we rely on the Holy Spirit to reveal things in our past that our memories and mental efforts have been unable or unwilling to detect or heal. Often, a wounded person will spend years with counselors, unsuccessfully trying to take away the deep-seated pain. Until the Holy Spirit reveals a secret heart attitude, often locked away in a childhood trauma, the person will not find freedom.

If you have never repented of your sins, ask Jesus to forgive and cleanse you from all unrighteousness and invite the Holy Spirit to live within you and be your Counselor. You can do that right now by praying this prayer:

"Jesus, I acknowledge that I am a sinner and can never earn my way to heaven. Thank you for dying for my sins on the cross. I repent and turn away from all my sins and invite you to be my Lord and Savior. Come and live in my heart through the Holy Spirit. Amen."

Wounded Hearts

How is it that our hearts get so wounded? Heart wounds can only come from people that our hearts are open to. If a stranger were to walk into your room today and berate you, you would laugh it off and quickly forget it. But if your mother or someone close to you, said those same words, you would be devastated. The expression "Sticks and stones may break my bones, but words will never hurt me" is not true. It is often easier to recover from a broken bone than from hurtful words that were spoken to us from someone we love and trust. You might have a scar on your body that came as a result of childhood injuries that you could now touch and talk about without feeling pain. When our hearts are scarred, it is often a different story. The deepest wounds anyone ever receives come from parents and siblings because they occur early in our lives while we are yet young, innocent and trusting.

CHAPTER 1
FAMILY RELATIONSHIPS: MOTHERS

Our first relationship is with our mother, and that relationship sets the stage for all other subsequent relationships. The relationship we have with her, from the moment of our conception, is a dependent one. What she eats, how she takes care of herself, where she goes, her relationships, her emotions—all these things have a direct effect upon us. She teaches us the language that we will use for the rest of our lives. We learn lessons from her even before we understand words. As a baby, we form our sense of value and worth by the way she feeds us when we are hungry, loves and holds us when we are afraid, and changes our diapers when they are soiled. We feel valued when she responds to those needs and comes when we call.

When we are young, we may not understand the words *loved* or *valued*, but we can feel them in her gentle touch or see them in her smile. We may not understand the words *anger* or *rejection*, but we can sense them in the tone of her voice or see them in her frown. If a mother does not feel that she is loved or valued, it may be very difficult for her to teach her children that they are valuable and treasured. Sometimes it is not what our mother did or said that hurt us, but rather the "vitamins" she failed to give us through her lack of nurturing.

Ron's Story

The first time I saw Ron, I felt the Father's love for him but recognized that something was wrong. He was such a servant of the Lord and had such a heart to bring God's love to the nations, yet he had a dark secret that kept him in bondage. With his eyes filled with tears, he confessed to me that he was full of rage that flared up at his wife and teenage daughters. He had beaten them on more than one occasion, but it had recently become so bad that it could no longer be hidden.

We prayed and asked the Holy Spirit to reveal whom Ron was angry at and any pain in his past that might have caused his anger. The Holy Spirit reminded him that his birth mother, who had conceived him out of wedlock, had given him up for adoption to a friend of the family. Next, he began to remember a deep betrayal of trust by his adoptive mother that happened when he was a teenager. As he remembered these things, he raged against both of them and expressed his personal anguish. From that same raging heart, he was able to forgive both of them.

Several years later, we saw him and his wife at a conference. With smiles on their faces, both reported that the rage and beatings had long since stopped, and their marriage and daughters were doing well.

God's Perfect Plan for the Family

It is God's plan for a couple to marry after a courtship or dating period in which they choose to remain sexually pure. It is also His plan that the marriage is blessed and approved of by both sets of parents and that both partners leave their mothers and fathers and cleave to one another out of love and trust, not out of rebellion or anger.

In this setting, a baby is conceived, and he is loved and rejoiced over from the first moment the couple learns of the pregnancy. The baby is born into a loving, peaceful and safe environment; and his birth is a celebration for the whole family and community. Mother and father care for and nurture the baby. When he cries, he is fed, changed, comforted and played with. He grows up knowing and believing that his world is a warm, safe place. He learns he can trust and submit to godly authorities because they are training him in the ways of the Lord and helping him to find his way according to his gifts and personality. He first learns to trust the softness of a woman from his mother and the strength of a man from his father.

Sam's Story

Sam called and asked to meet with me, stating he had a problem he wanted to discuss in private. Sam was ten years into his second marriage to a Christian woman and had several grown children of his own. He was employed in a physically demanding trade and was very masculine. Nothing about him classified him as effeminate.

Though it was very hard for him to say the words, he finally admitted that he struggled with bisexuality and a compulsion towards cross-dressing. During our meeting, we invited the Holy Spirit to reveal any pain in Sam's past that He wanted to heal. The Holy Spirit took him back to when he was a little boy, about six years old. At that time in his life, his brother contracted a terminal disease and died an agonizing death over a period of months. While Sam was reeling from the loss of his big brother, his parents emotionally withdrew from him. To deal with their pain and fear, Sam's parents threw themselves into their jobs, and he was often alone. Little Sam felt alone, abandoned and rejected. In the absence of healthy parental love, two things happened in his life. First, an older neighborhood boy molested him. Sam enjoyed being touched and "loved" by someone. Second, he began caressing and then secretly putting on his older sister's soft, silky feminine clothes, which reminded him of how it had felt when his mother held and comforted him.

The Holy Spirit brought up all the rage Sam had toward his parents for withdrawing their love from him. In times of stress, he had an overwhelming urge to dress up in women's clothes and find a man to comfort him. He hated himself for doing it later, but the compulsion just would not go away. After Sam expressed the anger and forgave his parents, the compulsion left and has stayed away for many years.

We will discuss this more in a later chapter, but from this story you may be able to see how Sam's mother taught him, through her emotional abandonment, that there was something wrong with or bad about him.

Learning Trust from Our Mother

In Psalm 22:9-10, David said that he learned to trust God by being able to trust his mother.

> *Yet You are He who brought me forth from the womb; You made me trust when upon my mother's breasts. Upon You I was cast from birth; You have been my God from my mother's womb.*

We are taught either to trust or to distrust by our early childhood parental experiences. Relationships are all about trust. Our parents are like gods to us when we are little children. For all we know, whatever they say is the truth, and it is those "truths" we build our lives upon. For example, they teach us that one plus one equals two. They teach us our alphabet and how to tie our shoes. And we believe them. So if they tell us we are stupid or smart, talented or worthless, we believe that too. If our parents (the ones who know us the most deeply) reject us, then we expect that others will also reject us if we let them get to know us deeply.

Let me tell you two different stories of how a lack of a mother's love and nurture can affect a child.

Jerry's Story

Jerry was one of the most polite, considerate men you would ever want to meet, but he struggled with a deep-seated belief that no one really loved him. He related a story told to him by his older sister about his life when he was a toddler. At that time, their father was a long-distance truck driver, and their mother worked nights to make ends meet. If Jerry cried at night, it was his big sister, not his mother, who was there to comfort him. As his mom slept during the day, he would be left in his crib, usually hungry or dirty. When he cried, nobody came, so why cry?

As an adult, Jerry did not ask for help from anyone. If he was feeling sick, he would get in bed, close the door and give instructions that no one touch him until he was well. He did not want to need anyone. His wife felt left out.

Her desire to be close scared him. What if he allowed himself to truly need her, and then she abandoned him? His mother taught him that no one really loved him. In fact she once screamed at him that he was unlovable. So he built his life on this foundational "truth." But is it God's truth?

Mothers are supposed to demonstrate and allow us to experience the unconditional love of God. Through this we should feel that no matter how badly we mess up, God and mother will always love us.

Karen's Story

Through most of Karen's young life, her mother, in an effort to medicate her own emotional pain, was on drugs. Karen's earliest memories are of taking care of herself and her little sister as their mother lay drugged in bed. At only four years of age, she remembers climbing on the kitchen countertop to get the cereal box down to make a meal for herself and her little sister.

Many times, she felt very scared as her mother drove wildly through the bad parts of town at night, looking for a drug dealer. After finding a source and taking the drugs, she would then drive home, even more wildly. Often, they barely escaped serious car wrecks as other cars blared their horns and swerved to miss them. She was too embarrassed to invite any friends over to the house, not knowing what kind of condition her mother would be in.

After having her first child out of wedlock and later going through a divorce that left her alone with a second child,

Karen came for counseling. She wanted to know what had propelled her into such a destructive pattern at such a young age. Through the Holy Spirit, she discovered that she had put a wall around her heart of rebellion in response to her mother's erratic behavior. Karen also wanted to know why she did not trust women. She said, "I trust men. They are direct. You know where they stand. Women are nice and soft one moment, and stabbing you in the back the next." For this reason, Karen avoided women's groups and, in fact, felt safest being alone. She had learned to distrust very early in her life, and it was hard for her to shake the feeling.

Splinters in the Heart

There is no deeper splinter in our heart than the one that comes from our mother. No mother is perfect, so we are not talking about one little misstep. However, if there is repeated damage to our child-heart, either by abuse or neglect, and it is never repented of to the child and healed, then we will probably need the Surgeon, the Holy Spirit, to perform heart surgery later in life. Hebrews says that the Word of the Lord is a short sword (*machira*) which is used for close, hand-to-hand combat. It can cut though the complex issues of our thoughts, emotions and motivations, or as the Bible puts it, our heart.

> *For the word of God is living and active and sharper than any two-edged sword, and piercing as far as the division of soul and spirit, of both joints and marrow, and able to judge the thoughts and intentions of the heart. And there is no creature hidden from His sight, but all things are open and*

23

> *laid bare to the eyes of Him with whom we have to*
> *do.* (Hebrews 4:12-13)

Bob's Story

Bob was a handsome young man whom I met while teaching a Bible study in the downtown area. I invited him to dinner with my family and to my church. He came a few times and then disappeared. The last time I saw him he told me, "When I was seven years old, I watched my mother beat my six-year-old brother to death with a baseball bat. I have a fear of women you cannot believe." He said he had been in secular therapy for twenty years.

Two years later, his picture appeared in the local paper as the new editor of a gay newspaper. A year or so later, there was an article telling about a gay doctor who had done research on gay men who had died, and the research showed that their brains were different from those of straight men. In the article, Bob was quoted as saying he had known since he was seven years old that he was gay. He did not mention the trauma he had experienced as a result of being a witness to the horrible abuse his mother had inflicted on his brother.

King David's Relationship with God

I believe that David learned to trust God by first being able to trust his mother and then his father. Since he was the youngest boy in a family of seven sons, his mother may have learned on the older sons and done her best mothering on David.

We must remember that David said, "You (God) made me to trust." Trust does not just magically happen. It is learned through positive experiences with people and God. Our trust and faith in God can grow or diminish based upon our life lessons.

Look at what David says about his relationship with God, which he also learned from his mother:

> *O LORD, my heart is not proud, nor my eyes haughty; nor do I involve myself in great matters, or in things too difficult for me. Surely I have composed and quieted my soul; like a weaned child rests against his mother, my soul is like a weaned child within me. O Israel, hope in the LORD from this time forth and forever.* (Psalm 131)

I think this psalm was written later in David's life at a time when, as a successful king, his life would have been complicated by managing several wives, many children and a vast empire. He was recalling a time in his childhood when he could climb into his mom's lap and she would solve all the problems that were too big for him. I believe David *knew* he could go to God in the same manner, and his God could solve anything. For David, it was not just a theory he had read in a book, but it was experience with his mother that he projected onto God. Do you think that might also have been a part of why David could trust God enough to go up against the giant Goliath? Do you wish you knew God like that? You can begin to discover that new relationship by allowing the Holy Spirit to go back, heal old wounds and remove lies that you have been taught about God, yourself, and life.

David also said that he saw his soul (or heart) like a child within him. Here he was a husband, father, leader of other men and ruler over a large nation. However, on the inside he was a little boy who felt overwhelmed by some of the things in his life. Many adults who are powerful people in one dimension of life can unfortunately act like little children in the way they relate to others around them. How many people have you known who were forty years old but acted like ten-year-olds and were very difficult to deal with?

Emotional wounds that happen in childhood often hold people hostage, even though we continue to grow physically and mentally. It is very difficult to have a deep, mature relationship with someone who is a little child at heart. By this, I do not mean childlike and trusting, but childish, selfish and self-centered. If we bring our wounded inner child to Jesus and let Him take the splinters out of our heart, we will begin to grow up and learn to face the issues we have been running away from like scared little children.

The fear of facing hurtful memories often keeps people away from those who could help them in the healing process--that is, until something happens that causes life to explode and results in a crisis that cannot be avoided. Before we are willing to ask for help, the pain of our situation usually has to outweigh our fear of being rejected if people really knew us. As is common to all of us, we do not look forward to surgery, even when we are in pain. We usually have to look at every other option first and be convinced that the surgery is necessary and the only answer. Until we reach that point and ask for

His help, the Holy Spirit (the Counselor and Comforter) waits patiently by our side.

Nathan Daniel

CHAPTER 2
FAMILY RELATIONSHIPS: FATHERS

Fathers, as much as mothers, teach us about God, life and ourselves. Jesus told us to address God as Father. If our earthly fathers were there for us and provided the love, discipline, support, and training we needed, we got a correct view of God. Just as mothers have the role of teaching us about the unconditional love of God, fathers have the role of teaching us how God wants us to grow up into our full potential. The Word says,

So the church throughout all Judea and Galilee and Samaria enjoyed peace, being built up; and going on in the **fear of the Lord** *(like a father)* **and in the comfort of the Holy Spirit** *(like a mother), it continued to increase* [bold and parentheses mine].   (Acts 9:31)

This is how our life experience with our mother and father should be. Our earthly family should show us unconditional love that tells us we are accepted in the family of God no matter how badly we mess up. It should also provide an environment where we are exhorted and expected to grow up, to mature, and to fulfill our call and purpose in the earth for the advancement of God's kingdom.

What if our fathers have repeatedly hurt us and never said they were sorry? What effect would that have on our lives? Scripture tells fathers in Colossians 3:21, *"Fathers, do not exasperate your children, so that they may not lose heart"*. Ephesians 6:4 says, *"Fathers, do not provoke your children to anger, but bring them up in the discipline and instruction of the Lord"*. In Ezekiel 18:2, we read, *"The fathers eat the sour grapes, but the children's teeth are set on edge"*. How many fathers have taken their anger out on and deeply hurt the hearts of their own children? These verses say that fathers can cause children to become exasperated and to loose heart, provoking them to anger and setting their teeth on edge.

Charlie's Story

Charlie had been struggling with a drug and alcohol addiction for twenty years. He wondered, "Why am I unable to kick the habit? What pain am I trying to numb with the drugs? What am I running away from?" As we asked the Counselor to come and show him any splinters in his heart, he remembered being disciplined by his father at the age of sixteen. His punishment was to mow the whole front yard, which was large, with a pair of scissors. He spent two weeks in the hot summer sun "mowing" the grass while his friends laughed at him. On another occasion, his father disciplined him by making him stay in bed for two solid weeks, allowing him to get up only to go to the bathroom.

A Father Teaches Trust

Fathers also play an important role in teaching us to trust. Through learning to trust our mother, we learn to trust the softness of the feminine. By learning to trust our father, we learn to trust godly masculinity and strength. So few people trust and respect those in authority because they did not have good, godly role models who were there to protect, to provide, and to be a positive example of doing what is right.

If we do not learn the benefits of trusting good, godly authorities and following laws, we will end up in a lot of trouble early in life. This is one reason so many youths are getting involved in gangs. They need the love and acceptance as well as the physical presence and masculine strength of a father who will tell them, "no," and will establish boundaries for them. Children will keep pushing until they finally find someone in authority who will consistently tell them the right thing to do, make them do it and discipline them if needed. Too often, without a father in the home, mom will give in and not make the child do what is necessary to grow up.

But what if that power is abused? What if our trust is betrayed? What if wrong lessons are accidentally or even purposely taught to us?

Joe's Story

I met Joe at a civic club I had joined. He was a well-known and respected local businessman in his early fifties. After I had the privilege of leading him to Christ, we began meeting for breakfast on a weekly basis. To help him grow in his newfound faith, he and I began reading the gospel of John together.

One night, I dreamt that Joe was having an affair and meeting a woman for breakfast at the very restaurant where we met to study the Bible. Since it may have been a warning of a coming temptation, I pondered the dream for several days before finally deciding to mention it to him. As I told him my dream, his face flushed. He then told me that he was indeed involved with a coworker, and they had met when and where I had seen them in my

31

dream. He also shared with me that, in addition to the affair, he had a secret life in which he participated in other forms of immoral activities. He was ashamed of his behavior but could not seem to resist them. We met together a few days later and asked the Holy Spirit to come meet with us and to go back in time and reveal any splinters in his heart that were causing the pain he was trying to medicate with his sexual addictions.

The Holy Spirit took Joe back to a time when he was six years old. His alcoholic father had placed him on the kitchen countertop and told him to "fall backwards, and I will catch you." Joe fell backwards, assuming his father's arms would be there to catch him, only to find himself crashing head first onto the concrete floor. As he lay there crying, his father said, "That will teach you an important lesson. Never trust anyone, not even your own father." Joe told me that shortly thereafter he discovered pornography and began to find comfort in sexual fantasy. Joe also told me that he thought the "life lesson" of not trusting anyone was so important and true that he had taught it to all of his children, who were now young adults. Do you think this life lesson had any effect on his relationship with his wife? Might that explain their lack of intimacy and his draw toward the false closeness of affairs and pornography?

Fathers and Daughters

A young girl is supposed to learn to relate to men in a healthy way through her relationship with her father. When he tells her she is pretty, hugs her with godly hugs, kisses her goodnight and praises her for helping mom with little brother, she has received positive feedback from the most important man in her life.

Her father then should be the "safe" man that she tries her feminine charm on. If he responds with affirming words and healthy hugs, she learns that positive, healthy men will be attracted to her and that she should expect the finest husband. Conversely, if the most important man in her life, who knows her best, rejects her and is never home or says hurtful things to push her away, she will get the idea that she has little value and may become vulnerable to any male who *says* he loves her yet only wants to use her.

Martha's Story

Martha was an attractive wife and mother. Her husband was a loving, faithful man, but it was hard for her to believe he loved her. Her own father had grown up in a terrible, abusive home environment. He enlisted in the military very young during a time of war and returned from the battlefield even more scarred. He met and married Martha's mother and they had several children. He was violently abusive towards all the children and his wife, and began calling Martha a whore when she was in grade school. His rages got worse every year, and Martha grew up watching him abuse her mother and brothers. One day when she was twelve, she found some makeup and spent an hour putting it on so she could show her dad how pretty she was. When he saw her, he asked how much she charged. Her angry response was, "Fine, then I will just give it away!" Over the next few years, she threw herself at many boys and young men who showed her attention or said they loved her.

God's design is that a godly father builds up his daughter during her early years by affirming and reaffirming her value. He protects and gently guides her, allowing her to make some choices but correcting her if her choices are *too* wrong. She eventually comes to a stage in maturity-- while she is still living at home--where she needs very little supervision, though it is always available. She has no reason to rebel, because she discovered long ago that dad's rules are only there for her protection and that anything that seems unreasonable is open for discussion. Since God's design for most women is marriage, this young woman will eventually leave the protection of her father's home and be blessed by a marriage to a healthy, gentle man with the same character traits as her father.

Because this young woman's heart was always open to her father, her husband enjoys the same trusting relationship. In Proverbs 31:11, we find a description of such a successful, blessed man: "The heart of her husband trusts in her and he will have no lack of gain." I was blessed to marry a pastor's daughter who had a wonderful, trusting relationship with her father. I was drawn to her not only because of her beauty and character but also because I could see the loving relationship she had with her mother and father and the warmth in her home. Her relationship with her father reminded me of the one Laura Ingles shared with her father on *Little House on the Prairie.* Because of the trust and respect my wife had growing up and continues to have for her father, her open heart went from her father's to mine without the pain that I so often hear married couples describe as they try to merge their hearts as one. When problems come up, my wife's heart response is to trust me and to assume that my intentions were right and good, which makes it so much easier to work through tough issues.

Fathers and Sons

It is the father's place to tell a boy when he has become a man in his father's eyes and to grant him honor as a young man. Fathers can easily communicate to their sons that they do not consider them to be masculine by making fun of them for not being mechanical or athletic or as physically strong as their friends. Just a few affirming words such as "I am really proud of the way you help with the yard work" or "I am proud of how hard you are studying, and I know you will be a good provider for your family one day" tells a boy that his father thinks he is measuring up to his father's definition of a man.

A father is to be a protector and a guide for his son, and he is to teach him to make wise choices in life. He should not take out his own hurts on his son or overly discipline him, which would make the son rebel. A father must not place too great an expectation on his son for his maturity. The father should keep an open, teachable heart towards the Lord. When he is wrong, he should ask his son's forgiveness for his wrong words or actions. This teaches his son that a man can be wrong, admit it and still be respected as a man.

Let me share with you a situation that happened in my own home. My three children, two sons and a daughter are now married adults with children of their own. As teenagers, my sons were creative young men who were involved in many projects that required the use of my hand tools. One day, a minor ten-minute repair I wanted to make to my wife's car took two hours because I could not find the right tool. As this was not the first time this had happened, I became very angry with my sons while they were away at school. Though I did not mind the messes they made, I did mind searching for tools because they had been left scattered and had not been returned to their proper place.

At this time, I had already been struggling with getting my sons to understand the importance of having a good work ethic and helping around the house while going to school and working part-time. Their perspective was that I was preaching at them too much, because they already knew these things. As a father, I saw things that they needed to have in their character before they were to establish a home of their own.

Because it was important to me that my sons have pleasant memories of working with me, I wanted to solve the problem in a positive manner. Before my sons came home, I asked my wife to help me discern if my anger was balanced and valid and to determine a solution that would not push them away. The solution we came up with was to buy each of our sons his own tool set and a third set for me that I could keep locked up and know things would be in their right place.

Now, years later, they are hard-working fathers who own their own businesses, and we enjoy working together on projects.

It is a father's role to find the difficult balance between *firm* and *flexible* and to know when to stand firm and when to bend. This balance must be rediscovered by each generation and modeled to the next.

A son will reach a stage in maturity where he needs little or no supervision, though his father will still observe his actions. The dad's advice, though not forced upon the son, is always available. The son knows and accepts most, if not all, of his father's *basic* values (based on Scripture) and will work out the less important ones on his own. One day, he will "leave his mother and father and cleave to his wife and the two become one flesh" (Genesis 2:24). He should not leave out of hurt and rebellion but because he has matured to where emotionally he no longer *needs* mom and dad. He is ready to discover his own identity, be an authority figure himself and answer directly to God for himself, his wife, and their future children.

In addition to physically moving out of the house, leaving home requires positive and healthy emotional detachment. Leaving out of rebellion, anger and hurt will prevent this from happening and result in negative emotional ties that will carry into the son's new home. Proverbs 31:28 gives an example of a young man who had a healthy relationship with his mother. Because of this, he sought a wife with character traits similar to his mother's, such as openheartedness, wisdom and kindness (Proverbs 31:11, 26).

As you can see, God's design for our life is often very different from the parenting most of us received. God can and will meet each of us where we are--today.

Nathan Daniel

CHAPTER 3
FAMILY RELATIONSHIPS: THE CHURCH

As mentioned earlier, deep hurt can come only from people to whom our heart, to some degree, is open. When we are born again, God places us into a church family. If you are part of a local church congregation, you are experiencing a little bit of what heaven will be like. Psalm 68:6 says, "God makes a home for the lonely." Relationships within church families can offer great love and healing.

One of Satan's greatest tricks to prevent the church from reaching out is for church members to accidentally or intentionally hurt one another. Since we enter into this family as a trusting spiritual baby, with our heart open and tender to others, we can be hurt by our new spiritual brothers and sisters. As was the case with my former associate, it can also happen to those who have been in the church for some time. When this occurs, many believers get so angry that they write off all Christians and walk away from all churches. They may even write off Jesus because of their hurts. If this has happened to you, do not be deceived. It is a demonic strategy to get your eyes and hopes focused on others and off the only perfect one, Jesus. If you are going to grow in the Lord and allow Him to use you, you will have to learn to forgive often and quickly and to keep your spiritual sword turned toward the devil instead of your brothers and sisters. Learn to outgrow the immature emotions you may be struggling with today.

When was the last time you got in a fight with a five-year-old? You will probably answer that it was when you were five. Do you think the person you are in a fuss with is petty, small and immature? One person told me, "You are as mature as the people you scrap with." In my own situation, I did not like to hear that because I considered the other person to be quite immature. If you truly forgive the person who has wronged you, you will outgrow him. You will also no longer be caught in the same type of struggle you are caught in today. **Learn to outgrow your enemies--forgive them!**

CHAPTER 4
ANGER

Handling our Anger

Without a doubt, one of the biggest insights I gained from the hurt I suffered at the church I was pastoring was that when I get hurt, I get angry. Even though I thought I had forgiven the man who had hurt me, I had only forgiven him on an intellectual level, and my heart had not caught up to my head in forgiving. As a pastor, I tried to act and talk as a more mature Christian and to be an example to others. I grew up believing that "good Christians do not get angry." This is very common for people who have been raised with a religious upbringing. It is most difficult to help people like me get free from their anger, because they are in denial of it. Non-believers and new believers are easier to help because they have not learned to hide their hearts. They will say, "I hate the jerk!" (or worse) and then let their anger out and forgive the abuser.

Jeremiah 17:9-10 says, "The heart is more deceitful than all else and is desperately sick; who can understand it? I, the LORD, search the heart." Before God can heal and cleanse our hearts, we have to come to Him and confess that we are sick of heart. I knew something was wrong with my heart and spirit, but I did not know what or why. I began searching the scriptures for answers to my bondage and discovered Leviticus 19:17-18:

> *You shall not hate your fellow countryman in your heart; you may surely reprove your neighbor, but shall not incur sin because of him. You shall not*

take vengeance, nor bear any grudge against the sons of your people, but you shall love your neighbor as yourself; I am the LORD.

The phrase "surely reprove your neighbor" means to be angry when he hurts you and to confront him. This scripture also says not to hate him or hold a grudge. God is showing us that He understands human nature. He is teaching us about our hearts and how to handle our anger, not deny it.

In my search for understanding, I also found Ephesians 4:26-27, which says, "Be angry, and yet do not sin; do not let the sun go down on your anger, and do not give the devil an opportunity." The New International Version of the Bible reads, "In your anger do not sin." Neither translation tells us to **not** be angry or to deny that we are angry. I have discovered that anger is a natural response to being hurt by someone who has access to our heart. If a total stranger said hurtful things, we would shirk off their words. However, if someone we love or respect does the same, we get hurt and angry.

Anger Due to Abuse

Mary attended a seminar on forgiveness that I was asked to teach to house church leaders in China. She had slipped in late and then gone into the bathroom to clean up and change clothes. Her friends told me later that she was homeless and working as a cleaning lady to take care of herself and her young daughter. Though she was a rather young woman, years of pain could be seen in her face. Mary's father had been a well-respected community leader and in a position of authority prior to the cultural revolution of the 1960's, but during that dark time in Chinese history the teenagers were allowed to and even encouraged to do very violent things to teachers, political leaders, business owners and anyone else who held a position of authority, honor and influence. As a result Mary's father would return home each day depressed and often beaten up. Mary's mother went into a deep depression and began experiencing a mental breakdown. Mary was the youngest of three children and was around ten years old at the time. Her mother began to keep all the windows darkened in the house all day to hide from the scorn of the neighbors, when previously they had been a well-respected family. Mary's mother decided to make Mary responsible for hiding and protecting all the family wealth in case something happened. Her father had invested all of the family wealth in precious jewels and diamonds, so her mother sewed the jewels into the hems of the clothes Mary wore to school each day, warning Mary never to lose one of them. This made Mary afraid to be a little girl and play with her friends at school, because her mother threatened to beat her if even one stone was found to be missing.

Mary's father gave her the job making sure that her mother took her psychiatric medications every day, which her mother fought taking. And then for some reason all the family teased Mary and told her that she was adopted. In China in the 1960's, many people would take their baby girls and abandon them in the countryside because they would rather have a son. They would literally lay them on the ground and walk off and hope their next baby would be a boy. Some people, if they wanted a "slave," would hear and see the baby crying, pick up one of these little girls and raise them, but then expect them to serve the family like a slave because they "owed" them their life. Because Mary's family treated her so badly, she often wondered if she really was their daughter, because she did not feel loved by them at all. When she was young she would often ask her relatives if she was adopted, and they would laugh at her, but she never got a straight answer.

As soon as Mary got old enough to marry and get out of the house she did so, and it was not long until she got pregnant and had her first baby. The baby turned out to be a little girl, so her mother-in-law told her husband to divorce her, for she was a bad wife because she had given him a girl and not a boy. So her husband divorced her, and now she was living on the streets, struggling to survive. In the meantime her father had reclaimed his favored position and wealth. Her parents and other siblings were living quite comfortably while she lived in poverty. Mary had recently become a Christian, but had never been told about the freedom that Christ offers us once we forgive from the heart.

We asked the Holy Spirit to bring up all her pain and anger so that she could forgive and be set free. She raged in pain and anger and then forgave her parents. She left our hotel room with peace in her eyes and heart. Two years later I got to visit her and her daughter, and she told me about being reunited with her parents and having peace in her heart towards them. They had finally given her their blessing.

When a Mother's Love Is Twisted

Jerry came to see me because his anger was out of control.

He was in his late thirties, married, the father of four daughters and a Christian. It seems that while in a rage, he had thrown his wad of keys down on the kitchen table. The keys had slid across the table and hit his two-year-old daughter in the face. The emergency room doctor suspected abuse and had called Child Protective Services.

In our counseling session, Jerry said he realized he had an anger issue but did not know where it stemmed from. We prayed and asked the Holy Spirit to come, go deep into his heart and show him the source of his anger. Suddenly, he remembered being nine years old and falling asleep on the living room couch while watching TV. He awoke to find his mother, drunk as usual, lying on top of him. She was wearing a bathrobe, but it was open at the front so her naked body was directly touching him. After that night, he became fascinated with girls' bodies. He remembered numerous occasions when he tried to touch his older sisters or their visiting friends while they slept.

He now knew the source of his anger toward women and understood that his mother had taken away his sexual innocence and awakened a nasty giant in his life. He hated his addiction to pornography and did not understand why he was powerless to stop it. Just a year prior to our meeting, his mother had died of cancer. He told me of going into her hospital room alone and quietly asking her, "Mom, did it really happen, the night you laid on me?" It was like a bad dream. His mother turned her back to him and died.

Anger Due to Neglect

We can be hurt by words or actions, but we can also be

hurt when people who are supposed to meet certain needs in our lives fail to do so. It is much easier to heal a wound about which we remember the circumstances than it is to measure a void in our lives.

Andy remembered at age thirteen slipping out of his house in the evenings. He would go down the street to the home of a friend who had a large, happy family. He would hide under their front porch during the summer months, just to listen to the sounds of their family being together.

Another man told me of watching the television show *The Waltons* and crying, wishing his family was like theirs.

Anger at something that *did not* happen is difficult to identify. We do not even know what we are missing, but we know we are missing something vital, especially when we compare ourselves to others who are filled with joy and confidence while we walk in fear and rejection.

When neglected in this way, we lack an emotional building block that we should have received when we were in our formative years. As an adult, we instinctively know that the void cannot be filled by anyone. The Holy Spirit however is able to lead us into healing and wholeness regardless of our age.

Greg's Story

Greg was having trouble in his marriage. He and his wife could never resolve their problems, because whenever things got stressful, Greg would hide behind a silly, childish grin and become silent. It was as if Greg disappeared behind a clown face. He wanted to grow and change, but something was blocking him. When we met, we asked the Holy Spirit to go back and see if there was anything that needed to be healed. Suddenly, he remembered being back in the second grade, chasing the other children around the playground because they were making fun of him and calling him "Stinky." He remembered that he looked odd because of the way his mother dressed him and cut his hair, and he smelled because he was rarely bathed at home. To hide his pain, he hid behind the nickname and put on a silly clown face. He pretended to enjoy the game that kids play in which no one wanted to be touched by him and thereby get the "cooties." As a result, Greg hated who he was and blamed himself for being too stupid to know how to dress, bathe and comb his hair in order to fit in properly at school.

When my co-counselor explained to him that at seven years of age these things were his mother's responsibility, Greg cocked his head sideways and said, "Really? I thought it was my job. I hated me then and still expect people to reject me today." As a child, Greg had been angry and had turned his anger inward. It really should have been directed toward his mother, a bright but selfish woman who had neglected him in some very important ways. As Greg expressed his pain and anger and then forgave his mother from the heart, he no longer found the need to blank out and let "Stinky" take over during stressful conversations with his wife. They began to be able to work through issues that needed to be resolved.

Nathan Daniel

CHAPTER 5
SUBTLE FORMS OF ANGER

Bitterness: The Cold Case File

John was sent by his pastor to see me. He was a faithful member of a local congregation, but he struggled with deep depression. His pain was so evident that it could be seen in his eyes. He was in his fifties, but he looked as tired as someone twenty years older who did not have any joy.

To prepare for our session, I had given John a book to read. As he sat down in my office, he said, "If this does not help me, I am committing suicide." I asked the Lord for guidance regarding what to say or do. I felt led to take the book, hurl it against the wall and say, "This isn't psychology; this is the Lord meeting us today." Then we prayed and asked the Holy Spirit to come minister to John. The Lord reminded him of his father divorcing his mother and abandoning the family. As a result, they experienced severe poverty and suffered the shame of divorce, which was still so uncommon in the 1940's. He was angry with his father for rejecting them.

When John was twenty years old and had been married for only one month, his father showed up at the apartment John shared with his new bride and asked to stay a while. A few days later, the newlyweds awoke to find that his father had drunk himself to death on their couch. John's young bride could not handle it and divorced him and his "crazy family." He bent over and wailed in pain. I led him in a simple prayer forgiving his father for rejecting and abandoning him and killing his first marriage. He had been carrying that old anger around in his heart for over thirty years. Old, cold anger not expressed as rage is called bitterness. It is not a violent outburst but rather a slow killer of the heart. After John forgave his deceased father, he said, "Wow, that knot in my gut is gone after thirty years." His pastor called to tell me what a changed man he was.

Contempt

There is an interesting passage in Matthew 5:21-26 which says,

> *You have heard that the ancients were told, "You shall not commit murder" and "Whoever commits murder shall be liable to the court." But I say to you that everyone who is **angry with his brother shall be guilty before the court;** and whoever says to his brother, **"You good-for-nothing," shall be guilty before the supreme court; and whoever says, "You fool," shall be guilty enough to go into the fiery hell.** [bold mine]*

Since Jesus said this in His "Sermon on the Mount," we must assume it is very important. What does it mean? Let us notice some things.

First, it says that if we are angry with our brother we are guilty before the court. I do not know of any country that puts people in jail for the emotion of being angry if they have not done or said anything that is against the law, so Jesus must have been talking about a spiritual court. Second, let us look at the words that He is concerned about. Calling someone "good for nothing" or "raca" (NIV) puts us before the supreme court. To call someone "fool" makes us guilty enough to go into the fiery hell. That seems to be a harsh sentence for what seems to be a minor crime in our estimation. What did Jesus want to reveal to us here?

When we keep anger in our heart toward someone who has hurt us, it can come out of our mouth in the form of contempt. The word *raca* in today's language would be translated "idiot," which refers to a person who might **not** know any better but does something that hurts us. The word *fool* refers to a person who **does** know better and still chooses to do something that ends up hurting us. In both cases, we are looking down on that person. We may not have an explosive anger towards him. We may, in a cold manner, distance or remove ourselves from him, but this is still contempt and anger.

Contempt for Women

Often, men who have been deeply hurt by their mothers have a deep-seated contempt for all women and see them as weak creatures that need to be controlled, not trusted. They cannot help but let derogatory or otherwise demeaning expressions come out of their mouths when dealing with women.

I remember well the day Will walked into our church with his wife and three small children straggling behind him. Will worked as a security guard and was fanatical about martial arts. He was skilled at computers but struggled to provide for his family as a security guard instead of pursuing employment in the field of computers. Three things stood out when you met Will. One was the hunting knife he carried in its sheath on his belt. The second was his unkempt appearance, which was accompanied by a strong body odor that pushed you away. The third was his glass eye. His wife and kids looked and smelled as if they lived on the streets.

Motivated by a conflict with his wife, Will came to counsel with me. As we prayed and asked the Holy Spirit to find the source of Will's ongoing struggles with his wife, the Holy Spirit, who is the Healer, took him back to when he was seven years old. He remembered his mother calling him into the house. When he went in, he found that not only was she her usual angry self, but she was in a rage. All he could remember was her grabbing his head with one hand and gouging out his eye with the thumb of her other hand. In just a second, his eye was gone. In the emergency room, she told the doctor some phony story and thereafter told everyone what a liar her son was about everything, so that no one would ever believe his side of the story.

Will harbored such anger towards his mother that he would not call her "Mom" but addressed her as "Hey, you." He even refused to consider her as a human, instead referring to her as "it." He had contempt for all women, and because of this, he kept his wife very much under his control. She was a bright woman but went around like a slave with her head down, rarely looking anyone in the eyes. Incidentally, Will told me that his mother had been very abused by her father and older brothers, once being thrown out of a two-story building by them. Her hatred of men came from the abuse she had received from the men in her family and then had passed on to her son.

I believe Will embraced martial arts so fanatically because of his fear and distrust of life in general, which also explains why he stayed in the security guard business and kept his knife on his side at all times. I talked to him about the freedom the Lord would give him if he were willing to forgive his mother. He refused to do so and stayed a prisoner to his anger and contempt.

Do Not Let the Sun Go Down

As mentioned earlier, Ephesians 4:26-27 says, *"Be angry, and yet do not sin; do not let the sun go down on your anger, and do not give the devil an opportunity."*

What does *"do not let the sun go down on your anger"* mean? Have you ever noticed that when you are first angry with a person or situation you can feel the stress in your body? You may want to punch something or someone or to shout and scream, but you **feel** the stress in your body. If you go to sleep, you probably will not feel the anger as much, or at all, the next day. You may then think that the situation was not that big of a deal, so you do not talk to the person in order to try and resolve the problem. However, the splinter in your heart has already begun to fester. Unless you truly forgave the person, you have "stuffed it." This is how walls begin to be built in a marriage and how churches split apart--one stone at a time. It is important to talk about, confront and resolve the things that have hurt you.

This is exactly what the phrase *"do not give the devil an opportunity"* is referring to. The Greek word for opportunity is *topos*, from which we get the word *topography*. Let us think about what this means.

53

Scripture is saying that if we do not resolve things very soon one way or another when we get hurt and angry, then we are **giving** the devil a right to have a geographical place, or real estate holding, within our heart. It is important to note that this passage was written to Christians—those who already have given their hearts and lives to Jesus.

Please let me emphasize this very important principle: Christians can **give** the devil an opportunity, stronghold or place in their lives. Christians, by not quickly forgiving others, can give the devil a legal right to have access to their heart.

There is another interesting passage in Matthew 18:21-35. Here is the story.

> *Then Peter came and said to Him, "Lord, how often shall my brother sin against me and I forgive him? Up to seven times?" Jesus said to him, "I do not say to you, up to seven times, but up to seventy times seven. For this reason the kingdom of heaven may be compared to a king who wished to settle accounts with his slaves. When he had begun to settle them, one who owed him ten thousand talents was brought to him. But since he did not have the means to repay, his lord commanded him to be sold, along with his wife and children and all that he had, and repayment to be made. So the slave fell to the ground and prostrated himself before him, saying, 'Have patience with me and I will repay you everything.' And the lord of that slave felt compassion and released him and forgave him the debt. But that slave went out and found one of his*

fellow slaves who owed him a hundred denarii; and he seized him and began to choke him, saying, 'Pay back what you owe.' So his fellow slave fell to the ground and began to plead with him, saying, 'Have patience with me and I will repay you.' But he was unwilling and went and threw him in prison until he should pay back what was owed. So when his fellow slaves saw what had happened, they were deeply grieved and came and reported to their lord all that had happened. Then summoning him, his lord said to him, 'You wicked slave, I forgave you all that debt because you pleaded with me. Should you not also have had mercy on your fellow slave, in the same way that I had mercy on you?' And his lord, moved with anger, handed him over to the torturers until he should repay all that was owed him. My heavenly Father will also do the same to you, if each of you does not forgive his brother from your heart."

Jesus tells us our heavenly Father will put us in a type of prison and turn us over to "torturers" if we do not forgive a brother "from the heart." That is tough stuff. However, I was in a prison like that for two years, and I can attest that it was real. It was a physical, emotional, psychological and financial prison, complete with torturers that visited me. They would come and go, and they loved to ruin a perfectly fine day.

For example, a year after I was "injured," we took a family vacation and went camping on the beach in San Diego. While there, my seven-year-old daughter and I were taking a walk on the beach at sunset. She was enjoying herself, skipping and humming as we walked. I was in a cloud of depression while replaying the "incident" in my mind. My daughter asked me, "Dad, what are you thinking about?" I was not going to lie to her. She could tell my mind was far away. So even though I was embarrassed that she had noticed my distraction, I told her truthfully, "I'm remembering someone who hurt me." She said, "Why are you thinking about that? Why not think about the birds, the sand, and this beautiful day?" And the Holy Spirit, my counselor, said to me, "Yes, why aren't you thinking about those nice things?" I guess I was enjoying my prison of bitterness and anger—my private pity party.

Years ago, while looking for property for our church to purchase, I saw an interesting ad in the newspaper for four acres of land. It read "a lovely place for a church." I called and made an appointment to meet the owner, who lived next door to the acreage. When I knocked on the door, an elderly man, pushed by a nurse in his wheelchair, came out of the house to meet me. He was tall and gray, and though his face reflected the extreme pain he was in, he had a friendly disposition. In our conversation, he told me he was a Christian. He also told me how he had come to California when he was a very young man, and he bragged about the properties he owned all over the county. After a while, I asked him about his health, and he told me he had had shingles for the past two years. I asked him if anything traumatic had happened around the time of the onset of the shingles. He said that indeed something had happened and went on to tell me how his son and grandson had conspired to steal one of his properties from him, how much he hated them for it and how he would never forgive them. He said it with rage and fire in his eyes, and then he screamed out in pain as the shingles stabbed him again. His last words on the subject were, "I will never forgive them! I will hate them until the day I die!"

You do not have to be behind bars to be in a prison; however, the key to your cell is your willingness to forgive from the heart.

Taking Back the Devil's Real Estate

The following is the testimony of a friend of mine who is a missionary. His marriage and ministry were in a crisis because of his bondage to pornography. He desperately wanted to be free from this snare but did not understand the correlation between childhood wounds and his addiction. Here is his account, entitled "My Two 'Father' Wounds," exactly as he wrote them to me.

> "The first wound occurred when I was four years old. At Halloween, my father insisted that I dress up as a girl (complete with a wig, makeup, dress). I vividly remember protesting and crying repeatedly that I didn't want to do it, but my Father wouldn't listen to my protests. He dressed me up and then took me out trick or treating, eventually bringing me to my kindergarten teacher's house, where I felt completely humiliated.

> As I reflect back on that wound, I believe that my struggle from adolescence to adulthood regarding passivity/ compliancy was partially due to this event. I believe that I "lost my voice" that day, giving up my right to argue or 'stick up' for myself, believing that 'what I really wanted' or 'what I really felt' wasn't important. I believe that

humiliation episode also greatly undermined my self-confidence and instilled in me a fear of bullies (a distorted Father image that I've had to also address in my thinking).

The second memory (7-8 yrs old) encompasses about 5 seconds of a mental clip that I played repeatedly in my thought life. I was sitting on the end of the sofa, watching one of my sisters walk across the living room, passing by the chair where my father was sitting. He reached his arm around her waist and pulled her into his lap and cuddled with her. I distinctly remember thinking, "I wish that was me." I didn't cognitively realize until 2000 (at age 39) that I had absolutely no memories of ever being hugged, kissed, or having received any kind of physical affection from my father. There was a huge need for receiving healthy affection and affirmation that simply never occurred.

I believe that as a boy, I was deceived by Satan into thinking that 'I was unlovable'. My father never told me that, but it felt true (emotionally) even though I could deny it intellectually. It became an 'operational lie' in my thinking and behavior. I remember looking into the bathroom mirror every day (sometimes multiple times/ day) as a teen and young adult silently asking my reflection, "Why won't anyone love me?" Following my marriage, those affectional needs were reduced greatly, but occasionally would flare up during times of extreme stress or anger, resulting in secret fantasy and masturbation. I believed it was my wife's role to love me and affirm me, but my extremely low self-confidence (and fear of rejection), and strong tendency towards passivity hindered me from being able to express these feelings. The truth is, I wasn't even able to articulate those feelings.

Years later while living overseas and in the stress and anxiety of culture shock, I was sucked into the secrecy and 'safety' (from rejection) of internet pornography and the resulting fantasy and masturbation. My freedom originated in the prayer ministry that I received from Nathan which involved forgiving my father, and releasing him from the debt that he owed me. I was also released 'from the tormentor' that day as I forgave that debt and asked God to bless my father's life, as well as my own. My ability to continue to walk in freedom has involved many hours of reflecting and analyzing my thought life and resulting behaviors, taking thoughts into captivity, re-programming my thinking with the truth of God's word (e.g. that I am loved unconditionally, accepted, and chosen), which has resulted in renewal of my mind and behavior."

Now five years later he reports the following:

"Although there is still temptation, it feels contrary to my nature, and the over-powering compulsions that ruled my life previously are gone."

Nathan Daniel

CHAPTER 6
FORGIVING FROM THE HEART

How Do I Know if I Have Forgiven from the Heart?

One way we can know if we have *not* forgiven from the heart is if certain people can "push our buttons" and set us off. When I was angry with my former staff member, the slightest mention of him would put me into turmoil. Even though I hid it well and controlled my words and actions, just seeing a car like his brought on depression. If other people mentioned his name, I would speak negative words about him. When we truly forgive from the heart, God removes our buttons, and those people no longer have a hold on us. Even the memories of them and the damage they have done begin to fade and lose their hold.

If you have forgiven someone from the heart, you will remember the time and place that you were injured. You will also recall a time and place when you forgave them. You will have a burial site where "you buried the hatchet." Forgiving from the heart is an act of your will. You have the responsibility and the authority as a child of God to give to others the very forgiveness that God has given to you. That is the point of the story in Matthew 18:21-35. Jesus would not tell us to do something we did not have the power, through Him, to do.

Receiving Forgiveness So We Can Forgive

Perhaps you are reading this book and realize that you have never received God's forgiveness for your sins. How can you give to someone else what you have not yet

61

received yourself? The Bible says that every human being has a sin nature and has sinned by choice. Jesus came to earth and lived a perfect, sinless life. He was God living in a human body. He did not deserve to die, but God allowed Him to be crucified. When He died, God placed upon Him the sin of every person that had ever lived or would ever live. By doing so, Jesus paid the penalty for all of our sins. God, therefore, offers each one of us a pardon for our sins. It is called forgiveness. We cannot earn it by being good enough. It is a gift called grace. Once we have received and experienced grace from God, then we qualify for heaven. We become God's adopted children. In order to continue in daily fellowship with Him, we have to be willing to forgive others who hurt us and give them the same grace that God has given us. That is called walking in the light. To walk in unforgiveness is walking in the darkness. God does not walk in darkness, so if we want to walk with Him we have to forgive others who hurt us.

Once we receive His forgiveness, we become His son or daughter, and our eternal relationship with God is secure. However, our fellowship with our Father can be greatly hindered if we will not obey Him. It will also be affected if we do not grow up in all ways unto Him and forgive as Jesus, our older brother, forgave those who sinned against Him. Paul describes this as "putting off the old self."

> *So this I say, and affirm together with the Lord, that you walk no longer just as the Gentiles also walk, in the futility of their mind, being darkened in their understanding, excluded from the life of God because of the ignorance that is in them, because of the hardness of their heart; and they, having become*

*callous, have given themselves over to sensuality for the practice of every kind of impurity with greediness. But you did not learn Christ in this way, if indeed you have heard Him and have been taught in Him, just as truth is in Jesus, that, in reference to your former manner of life, **you lay aside the old self**, which is being corrupted in accordance with the lusts of deceit, and that you be renewed in the spirit of your mind, and **put on the new self**, which in the likeness of God has been created in righteousness and holiness of the truth. Therefore, laying aside falsehood, SPEAK TRUTH EACH ONE OF YOU WITH HIS NEIGHBOR, for we are members of one another. BE ANGRY, AND YET DO NOT SIN; do not let the sun go down on your anger, and do not give the devil an opportunity.* [bold and capitals mine] (Ephesians 4:17-27)

God did not say *how* to do this, nor did He say that it would be quick or easy. In the "Lord's Prayer," Jesus taught His disciples to make the decision beforehand to forgive people who might hurt them by telling them to pray as follows: "and forgive us our debts as we forgive our debtors."

The Courtroom of Heaven

Chester was a tough-looking man in his forties who had spent years in prison shortly after high school. While incarcerated, he had come to see his need for God and had invited Jesus into his heart and life. He had been out for over ten years when he came to see me to discuss his pattern of challenging bosses and losing jobs on a regular basis. Because of his anger toward employers, his wife and kids often suffered the consequences of his unemployment.

When we asked the Holy Spirit to go back in time and deal with any pain that needed to be healed, Chester immediately remembered being terribly abused by his mother. She hated his father, who had deserted her before Chester was born. I led him in a prayer forgiving his mother for all the rejection and abuse.

The Holy Spirit also reminded him of a prison guard who had singled him out for extra abuse and had even turned the larger, older inmates against him and allowed them to do unspeakable things to him. Many times, he had been locked in solitary confinement for two weeks at a time for things that were not even his fault. The guard had told him repeatedly that he was a failure and a loser and would eventually return to prison because, as the guard said, "Losers always return."

As the anger he held inside toward the guard came to the surface, I could see his muscles bulging in rage. He clenched his fists, pounded on his knees and cursed as he spoke to the guard. He **did not** want to forgive the guard. Though it had been twenty years since Chester had walked out of prison, in a very real sense, he was still locked away. The guard, Jerry, still held the keys, and his label of "loser" still stuck to Chester.

I told Chester to imagine a courtroom scene with the following players:

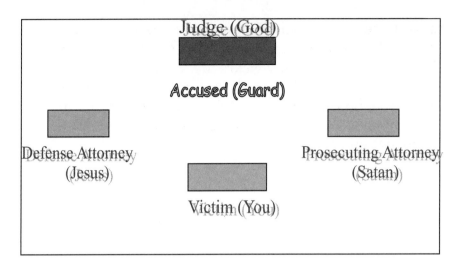

The Prosecuting Attorney (Satan) says to the Judge (God), "Do not forgive Jerry for the wrong things he did. Judge him harshly and send him to hell."

The Defense Attorney (Jesus) says, "Forgive him. Put his sins on My tab. I paid for his sins on the cross. Give him grace."

The Judge then asks the Victim (you, Chester), "What do you say I do to Jerry? Whatever you tell Me to do with him is what I will do with you! Should I forgive him or judge him harshly? Should I give him judgment or grace?"

It was not an easy decision for Chester to make. Jerry's label had hurt him deeply, and his curses had damaged his life. Chester struggled for several minutes, and then he made the choice with his will and pronounced Jerry forgiven, released and blessed. Immediately, Chester began to pray for Jerry's salvation. He realized that Jerry must have been a small man emotionally to delight in hurting him and putting him down. Chester also realized that spending so many years in such a depressing job must have taken a toll on Jerry. As soon as Chester set Jerry free, he himself was set free. His wife called me the next day and said, "Wow, what a change there has been in my husband!"

CHAPTER 7
WAYS TO FORGIVE FROM THE HEART

There must be as many ways to forgive people from the heart as there are different personalities, cultures and types of hurts to forgive people for. Let me share with you some different ways that have helped me forgive people.

1. Ask for Forgiveness.

The first way to forgive people is to do what God told me to do when I asked Him how to be released from my prison. God told me to personally ask my former associate, who had hurt me, to forgive me for hating him. God did **not** tell me to correct the man or to say that what he had done was all right. The reality was that I was guilty of the sin of hatred. In 1 John 1:9 we read, "If we confess our sins, He is faithful and righteous to forgive us our sins and to cleanse us from all unrighteousness." Because of my decision to obey and confess my sin of hatred, God forgave me and set me free. By the way, a year after I did this, the man who had hurt me resigned from the church. Within two years, he was no longer in ministry, and now twenty years later that church (which continued to hurt pastors) no longer exists. God did discipline him for his sins, but He waited until I had dealt with my heart first and had matured past him. By this I mean that I did not let his immaturity and pettiness hold back my growth and maturity in the Lord.

2. Bless the person who hurt you.

A second way is to make a commitment that every time you feel anger or are reminded of what the person did, you will get alone as soon as possible and pray aloud, "Father, in Jesus' name I forgive (name the person). I release and bless him, and I bless me too." God intends His people to be a blessing and to inherit a blessing. The devil wants to fill our fountain of blessing with anger, bitterness and resentment. In 1 Peter 3:8-9, it says,

> *To sum up, all of you be harmonious, sympathetic, brotherly, kindhearted, and humble in spirit; not returning evil for evil or insult for insult, but giving a blessing instead; for you were called for the very purpose that you might inherit a blessing.*

After I confronted and forgave my associate, I would see a car like his driving down the road. Suddenly, I would start feeling the anger and pain all over again. I would even start to replay the scenario of ugly things that my associate had said and done, and I would review all the consequences that had flowed out of the damage done to me. Before I even knew what had happened, I was feeling depressed and angry (both of which had almost become my normal, everyday moods). To counteract the anger, I asked the Lord to remind me to stop, get alone and pray that prayer of blessing on my former associate. There were times when I had to pray several times a day. This is what Paul meant when he said, "taking every thought captive to the obedience of Christ." In 2 Corinthians 10:5-6, the scripture says,

> *We are destroying speculations and every lofty thing raised up against the knowledge of God, and we are taking every thought captive to the obedience of Christ, and we are ready to punish all disobedience, whenever your obedience is complete.*

By my actions, I was choosing to make my mouth and will obey Jesus and forgive and bless my former associate. As I did so, the angry thoughts came less often and, finally, not at all. Now I never remember what he did except to tell this story to help others, and when I tell it there is no pain or anger at all. Years later, when I heard how his life had fallen apart and he was no longer in ministry, I was truly sad. I had probably prayed for him more than anyone else in his life. He may never have changed, but I did.

3. Write a letter.

A third way to forgive is to write a letter, **which you will not send**, to the person. As you write, tell them all the things they did or failed to do that hurt you. Express how you feel toward them. If you feel anger, say you are angry with them. If you feel rage, allow yourself to rage and even curse at them (if that is what is really in your mind). If you feel hatred or are bitter toward them, say you hate them. Bitterness is old, cold hatred, but it is still hatred. Read what Jesus said about hatred:

> *The one who says he is in the Light and yet hates his brother is in the darkness until now.*(1 John 2:9)

> *If someone says, "I love God," and hates his brother, he is a liar; for the one who does not love his brother whom he has seen, cannot love God whom he has not seen.* (1 John 4:20)

Writing touches the emotional side of our brain. Some people are able to bring up their anger because they "see" a picture in their mind of what happened in their past. For others, writing a letter helps them to get a hold of their anger. No one can do this part for us. Our assignment is to recognize our anger, and yet, in that anger, to not sin. The truth is most Christians are stuck in their anger because they deny it exists.

After you have taken plenty time to let the Holy Spirit bring up all the major things you feel you need to express, get alone and read the letter out loud to the Lord where no one will hear you. Let all the ugly stuff come out in whatever way your heart feels it. Be angry! After you have said it all, make the choice to say, "In Jesus' name, I forgive you." Specifically name each person and list all the things you are forgiving him or her for. Follow this by saying, "I release you, and I bless you." When you do this, the Lord will forgive you, release you from your prison and bind the torturers, in whatever form they may have taken. They may be evident in your life as physical pain (like the knots in my back), emotional pain (like my depression) or a sin addiction that you have not been able to get free from. Finally, bless them in every way you want God to bless you, and you will find that joy and blessing will begin to flow in your heart and life again.

When you have finished all these steps, it is important to destroy the letter. This will do two things: one, it will prevent any possibility that someone might find it; and two; it provides closure which is part of the "burial site" discussed earlier.

I was ministering to a young woman in China, who was a member of the underground church. We walked her through forgiving her parents who had neglected and abused her as a young child. We were counseling with her through an interpreter on the 28th floor of a skyscraper. I had her to write down on a sheet of paper each painful memory for which she was forgiving her parents. After she finished, I told her that when she was ready to forgive them she should tear the sheet of paper into tiny pieces and flush them down the toilet. I told her to envision the pieces of paper going down the pipes and far away from her into the sewer. As she did so, she was putting her parents' sins far away from her, just as the Bible says: "God will remove our sins as far as the east is from the west." As she returned from the bathroom, she had a radiant smile on her face. She was no longer held captive by these negative memories.

Why You Might Need Help From Others

> *Is anyone among you suffering? Then he must pray. Is anyone cheerful? He is to sing praises. Is anyone among you sick? Then he must call for the elders of the church and they are to pray over him, anointing him with oil in the name of the Lord; and the prayer offered in faith will restore the one who is sick, and the Lord will raise him up, and if he has committed sins, they will be forgiven him. Therefore, confess your sins to one another, and pray for one another so that you may be healed. The effective prayer of a righteous man can accomplish much.* (James 5:13-16)

A couple years ago, I was at a pastors' conference where the opportunity to receive personal ministry from a team of three pastors was offered to anyone who felt they needed it. I signed up because I remembered two incidents that had hurt me over two decades prior. I felt the hurts were hindering my ability to confidently lead my people as a pastor. I had struggled to deal with the issues and thought I had forgiven the individuals, though there was still some pain.

For over twenty years, I had been the surgeon for others, but now I had the opportunity to lie on the table and let someone else administer the healing knife to my life. I shared the two incidents with the men, and we asked the Holy Spirit to come and do His healing. I then prayed and asked the Lord to help me to open up emotionally because I knew I could go through the exercise in my head and go home with the splinter still in my heart. As soon as we asked the Holy Spirit to come, the tears began to flow down my face. I felt the emotions that had been locked away for all those years. As my emotions surfaced, I noticed that they blocked my rational thought processes. Even though I had helped many other people work through the same kind of hurts, my own emotional pain caused me to be confused and in need of someone else to guide my willing spirit to break free from the lies about me that had gotten lodged in my soul. The pastors helped me to walk through the healing prayers I needed to pray and renounce lies such as "I cannot grow a church; the people will not follow me." As soon as I prayed the prayers, the pain came out like a splinter. Over the next month, I as well as others in my church noticed a growing confidence in my leadership.

James 5:15 says to *"confess your sins to one another, and pray for one another so that you may be healed."* There are many things that we can work through alone with God, but there will be some things that are so deep within our being that God will allow us to need others to help free us. Perhaps the Lord allows this to show us that the Christian life is not a solo experience, but rather one that will require, by God's design, some degree of dependency on others. This verse also shows the relationship that can exist, at times, between sin and sickness. As in my case, my physical pain was directly related to my unforgiveness. I wish someone had been able to help me learn this lesson sooner.

How Do We Know What Is In Our Heart?

The words that come out of our mouth reveal what is in our heart. Matthew 12:34 says, *"For the mouth speaks out of that which fills the heart."* When you squeeze an orange, you get juice. Is the juice sweet or sour? The answer depends on what is inside the orange. What do you get when you squeeze a Christian? Whatever is inside: love or bitterness, peace or anger.

During the two years I was in my prison, the hurt and anger in my heart could not help but escape through my mouth. As much as I did not want my thoughts to drift to the injustice done to me, the conversation came around to that subject with almost anyone who seemed to care about me and might want to know my heart.

Just like an orange, whatever is inside us comes out when we are poked or squeezed. Others will experience sweet juice flowing out of us when we learn to forgive, grow past the people who have wronged us and draw on the availability of Christ's grace. When Jesus was being nailed to the cross he prayed, "Father, forgive them for they know not what they do." He instantly forgave them,

73

which is what He taught His disciples to do in the Lord's Prayer when He said, "Forgive us our debts as we forgive our debtors." He taught us to pray that *before* we get hurt.

One of the secrets of learning to *stay* free of anger and bitterness is to make the decision to forgive **immediately** after you realize you have been hurt. I love to do woodworking and sometimes get splinters in my fingers. I have learned that if I stop and remove the splinter immediately, it keeps the wound from getting swollen and infected, even though doing so hurts a little and takes time away from my project. If I delay in taking the splinter out, I will have more pain by the next day, and it will take longer to heal.

The Correlation Between Anger and Pornography

I have counseled many men with issues of hurt and anger and have repeatedly seen a direct correlation between unresolved anger and bondage to lust, pornography and/or masturbation. During the two years I was in bondage, I struggled with lustful thoughts like never before or since. The thoughts would go away after I repented, but they would repeatedly and frequently come back without provocation.

A recent statistic from a large evangelical denomination in America indicates that twenty-three percent of their pastors were enslaved to pornography. These men obviously love God and know His word, so how can they be in this bondage? I believe the reason is that many of them have unresolved emotional pain from childhood hurts, marital conflicts, or ministry wounds. Pain from issues related to their ministry could, in and of itself, create a stronghold in their life and give the devil a foothold or place in their heart. If the devil has a right to come and go in someone's life, it makes sense that he would bring his perverse thoughts and compulsions with him.

Over the last few years, I have been a part of a pastoral team that travels to different mission fields and hosts "Encouragement Conferences." Among other topics, the conference includes marriage seminars for missionaries. At every conference, we include a seminar on the thought life of the men. There is always a big response. Pornography is specifically addressed, as is forgiving from the heart. Over the course of time, the ministry team has seen many missionaries whose ministry and marriage were on the brink of destruction, and pornography was the symptom that exposed a deeper heart need. We have seen many of them learn to forgive someone who had hurt them, and *then* they were able to defeat pornography. Often the person they had to forgive was their mother. I have seen a direct correlation between a mother wound and pornography addiction.

I believe that pornography and masturbation provide a place of comfort and pleasure that feels "safe." A man can imagine a world where he is the center of attention. The woman is naked and vulnerable, and he is not. He can see her and feel intimate with her because of her nakedness, yet she cannot see him in his nakedness (who he really is) and reject him. This seems to satisfy a man for a short time, but without the fellowship God created him to need, the man is left feeling even more shallow and empty. He then pursues a brand-new pornographic image to look at on his computer. Often, a man who struggles with this addiction is afraid to really know and be known by his wife, because he is unwilling to risk the possibility of rejection. This is an issue not only with men but also with women, who tell me, "I have never let my husband into my heart of hearts." What a lonely way to live.

Cal was a young engineer who lived in the Northwest and came to see me while on a business trip. He was a single young man and quite handsome and had been a Christian for five years. He asked to meet with one of our healing teams because he was enslaved to pornography and was ashamed of it but could not break the addiction. When we asked the Holy Spirit to go back to any pain that might hold the power of the addiction, he remembered being in a home where he felt no love from either parent. His mother was gone working two jobs most of the time, and his father gave him the little attention he received. One day when he was about seven years old his mother walked in and found him playing doctor with the little girl next door who was six. He said his mother made them have sex and then said, "That's the only love you will ever know in this life." Shortly after this incident, he discovered his father's stash of *Playboy* magazines. His addiction to pornography and masturbation began at this point. He wept deeply as he forgave his mother and father for emotional abandonment and for his mother teaching him such a lie about sex and love, which she believed to be the truth.

Benefits of Learning to Forgive from the Heart

1. Forgiving from the heart gives you boldness in dealing with people. You will not be afraid to get close to them

and will have the ability to love them in a way you were incapable of before. Jesus showed us a perfect example in that He loved Judas even though He knew Judas was going to betray Him. In my own experience, I learned that forgiving people completely, no matter what they said or did to me, kept me from getting stuck emotionally in my heart. It was as if I now knew how to get out of a wrestling hold that had held me in its grasp for two years.

2. Once you learn to forgive from the heart, the Lord will allow you the opportunity to minister to others. He does not guarantee that you will not get hurt anymore. In fact, He will allow you to get hurt, so that through your ability to forgive, you will help teach others. He will give you eyes to see wounded people who need His healing touch. Have you ever heard the expression, "Hurt people hurt people?" In other words, people who have been hurt in life go around hurting other people who then need healing. By the way, hurting people are usually drawn to and marry hurting people, the result of which is often an explosive marriage. The Lord does not tell us to stay away from those who may hurt us but to discern that when we relate to them they will probably hurt us out of their own woundedness, so be careful and prayerful in dealing with them.

3. You will recover the power of focus. During the two years I was in my prison, I did not even realize how much time I had wasted trying to figure out what was wrong and how to prevent this kind of hurt from happening again. Since I got hurt in a political storm in a blue-collar church, I read books on how to organize blue-collar churches. I also thought my denomination may be the

problem, so I researched other denominations but found that very similar problems existed in them.

The reality was that the problem was due to sin and sinful human nature. In essence, I was trying to intellectually figure out evil so I could predict it, control it and prevent it from reoccurring. Many people will put up a guard, such as "All men (or women) will hurt you," to protect themselves from being hurt again. I firmly believe that much of the reason many young people are attracted to homosexuality is because of the wounds of abuse inflicted by someone (often a parent) of the opposite sex. In an effort to prevent the hurt from happening again, they put up a guard toward the opposite sex. Boys, because of a hurtful experience with their mother, often vow never to trust the softness of the feminine. Girls, if deeply hurt by their fathers, often make a similar vow never to trust the strength of the masculine. Homosexual relationships however are also far from perfect. They also wound each other out of *Eros* (the Greek word for selfish love).

When you are able to forgive from the heart, you will not need to put up a shield around your heart for protection. Instead, you will trust God to give you the grace to quickly forgive people and, in that, find that people are willing to quickly forgive you when you mess up. On the other hand, when you do not or will not forgive people who make mistakes, you do not have the right to expect others to give you grace and forgive you when you mess up.

Forgiving from the heart resolves that issue. You are no longer powerless, held captive by an abusive person, but you have decided to forgive him and to redirect your focus away from the abuse you allowed to dominate your life. Instead you make Jesus become the focus of your life. We become like the one upon whom we focus.

After I forgave, I discovered I could get things done so much faster because I could focus on the task at hand with the entirety of my conscious mind. My subconscious mind was no longer using fear and anger to rob and drain my mind and emotions with the injury that was two years in the past.

4.   You will enjoy *today*.   In my own experience, I remember living in the past and replaying the hurtful incident in an attempt to avoid such a problem in the future. I have already mentioned the occasion when I was vacationing with my family. My daughter and I were walking on the beach, and something triggered painful memories, yanking me back in time. My daughter asked me what I was thinking about. I replied, "I was just remembering how someone hurt me." She asked why I was thinking about that instead of the birds and the sea and the sky and the pretty beach. The Holy Spirit whispered to me, "Yes, why are you not thinking about the beauty that I created around you?"

Once you forgive from the heart, you will be free to live without fear and regret. You will live in today, not looking back and trying to correct the mistakes of yesterday. Living for today means trusting God to protect you every day. If He allows you to get hurt, it means He has given you an opportunity to grow up and learn to forgive like Jesus forgave.

5. You will have renewed power over your thought life. From discussions with other men who have been set free from lustful thoughts, my experience was not unique. The only way I can describe the difference is that for those two years, the thoughts were strong on the *inside*, and I had to fight them daily. After I forgave, they were on the *outside*, and I could easily keep the door closed because they had very little power.

Consider the following illustration: For many summers, I had locked only the front and back security screens at night, leaving the doors open in order to allow the cool breeze to blow through the house. Early one morning, I happened to see a little mouse squeeze through a small half-inch crack under the front screen and scurry across the floor into a closet. Once he was inside, it took many days and several mousetraps in various locations to track him down and get him out. From then on, I kept that door closed and opened only a window that was too high for a mouse to climb up into. Once we realize that we have accidentally opened doors to the enemy, we must do whatever God requires to close those doors in practical ways and keep them closed forever.

6. Forgiving from the heart removes your emotional buttons. Someone once said, "You are a slave to anyone that can make you lose your temper." Once we forgive from the heart, God removes our "buttons." If you are tired of certain people being able to say just a few key words and put you in emotional and spiritual turmoil, ask God to help you forgive them, and you will outgrow them, and their words will no longer be able to enslave you. You will find yourself smiling whenever they play their old tricks on you and they fail to rile you anymore.

CHAPTER 8
DETOURS ON THE ROAD TO FORGIVENESS

The Detour of Self-Deception

The Bible says that our heart is deceitful, and it tricks us into thinking we have been honest and have forgiven from the heart when we really have not.

> *The heart is more deceitful than all else and is desperately sick; who can understand it? I, the LORD, search the heart, I test the mind, even to give to each man according to his ways.* (Jeremiah 17:9-10)

For some reason, our heart wants to hang on to its right to judge and be angry. Like a stubborn little boy who does not want to forgive his brother and give him a hug, our heart can stubbornly hide and hang on to an offense. As adults we become adept at putting on a smile and shaking hands with someone we may totally distrust and disdain. This may even be a Christian brother, sister or church leader. I have discovered that the easiest people to help get free from anger in the heart are unbelievers or new believers who have not yet learned what they "ought" to do, think or feel. They will come in and say, "I am mad and want to kill them." Whereas, someone who has been a Christian for a while might say, "I do not like them as much as I like other people, but I do not hate them." The first step to forgiveness is being aware of and honest about what is in our heart. Written to believers, 1 John 1:8-10 says,

81

If we say that we have no sin, we are deceiving ourselves and the truth is not in us. If we confess our sins, He is faithful and righteous to forgive us our sins and to cleanse us from all unrighteousness. If we say that we have not sinned, we make Him a liar and His word is not in us. [bold mine]

God is not surprised that after salvation we still have things in our hearts that we need to work on. He has made provision for that.

The Detour of Excusing

Another detour we can take is that of excusing rather than forgiving. It goes like this: "When my mom was drunk she would say and do really terrible things to me. Even today, thinking about those things can make me cry. Sometimes I say and do some of those same awful things to my own children. I know that my grandma did those same things to my mom, so I really cannot be angry at her." That is excusing rather than forgiving. It also lets *us* off the hook for wrong behavior towards our own children.

God does not excuse sin, and He calls it what it is. Through Jesus, God endured suffering and paid the penalty for our sins by stepping down from heaven and dying on the cross. Now He calls upon us to share with Him in Christ's sufferings by forgiving those who sin against us.

Human nature finds it easier to excuse people than to forgive them. Forgiving does not say that what they did was right. Forgiving does not try to explain the behavior away. Forgiving says that what was done to us was wrong and sinful, but we choose to forgive the wrongdoer because God has forgiven us. We do not *deserve* to be forgiven by God, and others do not *deserve* to be forgiven by us. Explaining and excusing make the sin seem okay. God never winks at our sins, but when we come and confess that we are sinners and need forgiveness, then the shed blood of Jesus falls upon us, and He cleanses us. This is not because we *deserve* it, but because God graciously gives us what we do not deserve. This is grace. After we become a grace receiver, then we can become a grace giver.

People who have been hurt and have not learned to forgive from the heart are usually very judgmental people. They also have long memories and well-maintained lists of sins others have committed against them. You would not describe them as carefree and joyful.

Be honest! You are hurt and angry. There was no excuse for what they did. Now, forgive them, and then God will forgive and change you too.

The Detour of the Past Tense

If you acknowledge that there is hurt towards someone, a tendency can be to say that you hated that person. The word *hate* is used in the past tense, as if now things are on a right relationship. The truth of the matter is that there is still hatred and you are still angry towards the person, and that is the reason you still have the problem. If you had hated and then forgiven, you would no longer have pain in the memory when you talk about the incident. Along with that, there would be a burial site marking the point in time when you forgave, just as you have an injury site marking the point in time when you were injured.

I need to clarify that I am not asking someone to communicate with the dead or speak to the spirit of a person who is not present. The Holy Spirit is not limited to time as we are. He is able to help a forty-year-old person remember how she felt (and still feels) in her heart about someone who hurt her when she was five. He is able to bring up the pain that is hiding in her heart so she completely forgives in obedience to the Lord. Once I saw a big, husky senior adult man curl up like a three-year-old boy and say, "Bad Mommy!" as he relived the memory of his mother violently abusing his little brother who later died from the abuse.

CHAPTER 9
EMOTIONS

Learning About Our Emotions

When feeling a strong, negative emotion, we need to stop and name the emotion we are feeling. Identifying and labeling our emotions is important because it helps us realize that emotions are real; they are not just words we think.

Hatred is one such strong, negative emotion that needs to be identified. There are many scriptures that address hate:

The one who says he is in the Light and yet hates his brother is in the darkness until now. (1 John 2:9)

But the one who hates his brother is in the darkness and walks in the darkness, and does not know where he is going because the darkness has blinded his eyes. (1 John 2:11)

Everyone who hates his brother is a murderer; and you know that no murderer has eternal life abiding in him. (1 John 3:15)

If someone says, "I love God," and hates his brother, he is a liar; for the one who does not love his brother whom he has seen, cannot love God whom he has not seen. (1 John 4:20)

John, the apostle who taught the most about love, wrote these verses. This is of interest because he and his brother James, whom Jesus nicknamed "the sons of thunder," had at an earlier time asked Jesus for the power to call down fire and destroy a Samaritan city that would not sell them bread. Through these verses, we can see how John had grown and matured in his understanding of love toward others.

The Lord has shown me that all my emotions are either on the side of and possess the qualities of light and love (gentleness, kindness, patience, joy, mercy, and so forth) or of darkness and hatred (anger, hatred, bitterness, wrath, murderous thoughts, envy, rage, contempt, and so forth). The good news is that it is God's job to forgive me and cleanse me of all the darkness. The only thing He requires is that I drag the sinful emotions and responses into the light and agree with God as to what is in my heart. The Bible says in 1 John 1:9-10, *"If we confess our sins, He is faithful and righteous to forgive us our sins and to cleanse us from all unrighteousness."*

There is a world of difference between *admitting* sin and *confessing* sin. Admitting sin says, "Yeah, so I lied, so what? Big deal." Confessing sin says, "God, I am guilty of hating my brother. I am sorry, but I cannot change my heart. Please forgive me and change my heart toward my brother." Confessing our sin is coming into agreement with God about what He calls sin, not hiding or justifying it. Hanging onto my anger and hatred is never justified, no matter what my brother may have done. Even if my brother never repents or changes, I will benefit and grow from responding like Jesus did when He was treated unfairly.

Changing Our "Normal"

People who have been damaged emotionally for a long time view anger, bitterness and depression as "normal." It is a familiar feeling or condition. They do not even question these emotional states, though they do not really like or enjoy them.

I use this illustration: Occasionally, I will take a drive from my home in the city into the country. Along the way, there is a dairy farm with a large manure pile, the odor from which grabs my attention in a negative way. In comparison, a ranch hand does not even notice the smell because he has become conditioned to it. The point of the illustration is this: People who were raised in a home with fussing and fighting see it as normal. They do not like it but do not know any other way. After they forgive from the heart, their "normal" will be joy, happiness, cheerfulness, peace and love. In other words, they will be filled with the Holy Spirit instead of with their damaged and angry emotions.

When people get their hearts clean, they are surprised at how wonderful they feel in their spirit most of the time. This is their new "normal." It is important to recognize, however, that the enemy of our souls will try to get back in after the negative emotions are cleaned out. To prevent this, we should view anything that upsets our spirit as an alarm or warning to stop and ask the Holy Spirit what upset our peace. Not letting the sun go down on your anger means taking notice of your spirit and heart and asking the Lord to show you anyone you need to forgive. As soon as you take the steps necessary and pray the situation through, your peace will return.

87

Nathan Daniel

CHAPTER 10
WHAT FORGIVING FROM THE HEART DOES NOT MEAN

1. Forgiving from the heart does not require confronting the offender. Many people find themselves stuck with anger toward an aged or deceased parent. Even though the damage occurred many years ago, the adult child may still be struggling with the effects and consequences. If confronted, the aged parent might deny that the damage occurred or may reply, "You did not turn out so bad," or "Just wait and see how well you do with your kids." The following illustrates an effective way to deal with this unresolved anger.

Melinda's Story

Melinda was a single parent trying to raise three kids. Her middle son was autistic, which made Melinda's burden so much more difficult. While Melinda was growing up, her father was an award-winning educator in the Midwest, but at home, he was horribly abusive toward his own children. One incident Melinda related was of her dad forcing her oldest brother to eat his dinner night after night out of the dog's bowl beside the family dog.

Relationships were difficult for Melinda, to say the least. We all had to struggle to work with her in the church. She had an abrasive way about her that was almost as if she was itching for a fight. She dressed more like a man and acted tough in her speech and mannerisms. In counseling, I asked her to write a letter to her mom (who had stood by and let her dad harm the kids) and to her dad, telling them about all the pain they had caused her.

She also wrote how those things had contributed to the difficulty she had had in life and with relationships, eventually leading to her divorce. As she read the letter and forgave her parents, the Holy Spirit pulled out the painful splinter from her heart.

A couple of months later Melinda told me of a phone call from her parents. Her father said, "I do not know what has happened in you, but it is really good. Maybe it is that church you are going to. Keep it up. The changes are good." She told me that her dad had said a couple things that would usually set her off, but she felt no anger towards him. She realized that she had outgrown him.

2. Forgiving from the heart does not mean the other person has to say they realize they are wrong, apologize and ask for your forgiveness. Choosing to forgive from your heart does not necessarily mean you will ever be reconciled with the offender. You do not have to wait until anyone else changes in order to be set free from your prison of anger. You can forgive today, regardless of the other person's position or attitude. It would be ideal if there were complete reconciliation, but it is not at all necessary in order for your heart to be at peace with God and to have God's love for the person who hurt you.

3. Forgiving from the heart does not have to take years. Once you realize and confess that you still have anger and unforgiveness in your heart, and you are willing and wanting to forgive, even if only from selfishly wanting to be set free, then you can forgive quickly. Though it may still take some preparation to get the pain and anger up and out of your heart, forgiveness does not need to be a long, drawn-out process.

4. Forgiving from the heart may *not* occur overnight. It may require prayer many times a day for months before the battle is won. Some people are unable to get their stuffed anger to surface in an honest way and to forgive during one prayer session. Because they have stuffed and numbed their emotions for many years, they may be unable to change their emotional makeup in an hour.

Through my own experience, the Lord gave new meaning to 2 Corinthians 10:5, which says, *"We are destroying speculations and every lofty thing raised up against the knowledge of God, and we are taking every thought captive to the obedience of Christ."*

In my own experience, I had to learn to recognize when I became bothered in my spirit and, as soon as possible, get alone and ask God through prayer what it was. Doing so would require winding my thoughts backward through the day to remember what had triggered the negativity. When I realized the source of my agitation was the anger I still felt toward my former associate, I would pray for him. I would pray aloud so my ears, the Lord, the demons and the angels could hear.

I would ask the Lord to tell me different ways to pray blessings on him. I prayed every blessing on him that I wanted for myself. I did this for six months. Sometimes I had to do it several times a day. I remember being seated at a very special dinner at a friend's house when something was said at the table that reminded me of this person, and my spirit started being depressed and angry. I excused myself from the table, went inside the bathroom and slowly and quietly prayed the prayer aloud. I waited to return to the dinner table until God's peace came upon me.

By my actions, I was taking every judgmental and angry thought captive. I was also making my mind and will obey Jesus, who said, *"Love your enemies and pray for those who persecute you, so that you may be sons of your Father who is in heaven"* (Matthew 5:44-45). As I said earlier, I later learned that this man had left the ministry, his life in shambles. I was genuinely sad to hear the news. From my reaction, I realized my heart had truly changed, and I rejoiced.

Like Abraham, you and I, as sons and daughters of the King, have the power to bless.

> *And I will make you a great nation, and I will bless you, and make your name great; and so you shall be a blessing; and I will bless those who bless you, and the one who curses you I will curse. And in you all the families of the earth will be blessed.* (Genesis 12:2-3)

What a difference it makes in our spirit and mind to think about how to pray blessings on people as opposed to judging and cursing people in our thoughts and with our words. Proverbs 24:17-18 says, *"Do not rejoice when your enemy falls, and do not let your heart be glad when he stumbles; or the LORD will see it and be displeased, and turn His anger away from him."* We can also bless ourselves and expect to be blessed by God and others. In 1 Peter 3:8-9 it says, *"To sum up, all of you be harmonious, sympathetic, brotherly, kindhearted, and humble in spirit; not returning evil for evil or insult for insult, but giving a blessing instead; for you were called for the very purpose that you might inherit a blessing".*

To sum up these two verses it says we were made to **be a blessing and inherit a blessing**.

Indeed, my former associate needed to be corrected, but God waited to correct him until after I had learned my lesson and forgave him from the heart. Could it be that God is waiting for your heart to change first before he corrects or admonishes your enemy?

5. You do not have to wait until you really **feel** love for the person before you forgive from the heart. You can be motivated completely by your desire to get out of your own prison. If you do not like the pain, forgive! God will be just as happy no matter *why* you forgive, and you will be free. When you forgive and release someone, they are released in the realm of the spirit. In the earthly realm, this is similar to when a judge, because the law dictates a release, pardons or releases an accused or convicted person whom he might personally dislike.

Scripture says that we are seated with the Lord in the heavenly places and that we will one day judge the angels. As princes or princesses of the Lord, we have royal and spiritually legal authority. We can use this authority to judge and condemn (and therefore get judged and condemned) or to forgive and release (and therefore get forgiven and released). If we choose the latter, we will bless and be blessed.

Forgiving Yourself

Some people struggle with receiving grace from God. I

think this may come from a background where they were taught forgiveness, but grace was something that had to be earned or paid for through penance, such as crawling up a mountain on your knees. Grace, by its very nature and definition, is something given to someone who has made a mistake and does not deserve to be forgiven. God gives us grace that He Himself bought through the death of his precious Son, Jesus. Sometimes the thing we did was so bad or the consequences and effects on the lives of our loved ones were so huge that we just cannot understand how God can forgive us without punishment. As a result, we beat ourselves up repeatedly in our mind. As a pastor, I would sometimes criticize myself for not handling a person or situation in the best way. I would spend many hours in regret, wishing I could have another chance to try a different approach with that person. The Lord had to show me that beating myself up did not advance His kingdom at all. He wanted me to get off the sidelines, get back in the game, learn the lesson from my mistake, forgive myself and get up and try again.

When we receive God's grace and forgiveness, we will be changed so we can forgive others more quickly and easily. We also realize that we will again make mistakes, either innocently or intentionally, and need to be forgiven. There are times when others will be hurt by our actions and choices, even though we are acting as righteously as possible.

For example, you are forced to close a business that you own because it is failing due to a changing economy. All your employees will lose their jobs in a few months, but you decide it is best to close it as soon as possible to salvage the most that can be salvaged. The week before you announce the closure, your employee Fred buys a new car. Fred becomes angry with you because not only has he lost his job but he is worried that he may also lose his new car. It is not your fault, but Fred blames you. In closing your business, you have neither sinned nor intentionally hurt anyone. Though Fred is still angry with you and needs to forgive you, it does not mean you should not have closed your company.

If you are in the habit of really forgiving and not holding a grudge or writing people off, you can expect and will experience forgiveness from others when you make a mistake.

Nathan Daniel

CONCLUSION

You may come, like I did, to the realization that you are in bondage. You may be tired of exploding on your family and driving them away when you know they are not the source of your pain or anger. You may be in physical pain or suffering from depression. Perhaps you have already been to the medical doctor and have found out that neither surgery nor pills will bring you the relief you need. If any of these describe you, invite the Holy Spirit to minister to your heart right now by praying the following prayer:

Lord, I am hurt and angry. If there is someone I need to forgive, please show me who it is. Bring up the memories that hold the pain. I make the choice to forgive them, but I know that first I have to be honest about my anger. Help me be angry, Lord, so I can then forgive. Show me my sin as you see it. Show me my heart.

Now, I release (person's name) into your hands, Lord, and forgive them for all the offense(s) they committed against me. I ask you to come into my heart and cleanse me from all unrighteousness so I may walk in freedom through forgiveness.

Imagine living a life free of anger and pain. Congratulations! Because you prayed the prayer of forgiveness, you are about to experience such a life. You do not need to carry around a heavy coat of armor and a big shield, but rather you now have something better.

First, you have the ability to perceive wounded people by being able to see in their eyes the pain you used to carry in yours. You know to be careful with them as with any wounded creature that might bite someone who gets too close. You will be able to offer them the very freedom and healing they need.

Second, you have learned to free yourself of the wrestling hold of hurt and anger through the power of forgiving people. You will always be able to quickly forgive others from the heart and stay free, never to be tricked into staying in the prison of unforgiveness and bitterness. Peace, joy and love will be the "normal" state of your heart! Anytime you feel something affecting your peace and joy, stop and ask God to check your heart for splinters, and then forgive.

Is it not interesting that Jesus said in Matthew 7:5, "You hypocrite, first take the log out of your own eye, and **then you will see clearly to take the speck out of your brother's eye**"? [bold mine] After we let God deal with the anger and unforgiveness in our own hearts, we will be able to take the speck out of our brother's eye. I believe that, in time, others will come and ask us to help them experience the freedom that we have witnessed in our life. God bless you in your new life of freedom.

About the Author

Nathan Daniel is a graduate of Grand Canyon University and has a Masters of Divinity from Southwestern Baptist Theological Seminary. He has been a pastor for thirty five years and is the founding pastor of Grace Fellowship in El Cajon, Ca. He is married and has 3 married children and eight grandchildren. He ministers internationally to pastors and missionaries and is available to teach and train through seminars on Freedom Through Forgiveness. He can be contacted on the web at:
www.Freedomthroughforgivenessministries.com

SUGGESTED READING
Healing the Masculine Soul by Gordon Dalbey
The Bondage Breaker by Neil T. Anderson
Healing of Damaged Emotions by David Seamands

Nathan Daniel